IPv6 Neighbor Discovery

CSPress

Press Operating Committee

Chair

James W. Cortada
IBM Institute for Business Value

Board Members

Mark J. Christensen, Independent Consultant
Richard E. (Dick) Fairley, Founder and Principal Associate, Software Engineering Management Associates (SEMA)
Cecilia Metra, Associate Professor of Electronics, University of Bologna
Linda Shafer, former Director, Software Quality Institute, The University of Texas at Austin
Evan Butterfield, Director of Products and Services
Kate Guillemette, Product Development Editor, CS Press

IEEE Computer Society Products and Services

The world-renowned IEEE Computer Society publishes, promotes, and distributes a wide variety of authoritative computer science and engineering books, e-books, journals, magazines, conference proceedings, and professional education products. Visit the CS Store at www.computer.org/store to see the current catalog.

To submit questions about the books and e-books program, or to propose a new title, please e-mail books@computer.org or write to Books, IEEE Computer Society, 10662 Los Vaqueros Circle, Los Alamitos, CA 90720-1314. Telephone +1-714-816-2169.

Additional information regarding the IEEE Computer Society Press program can also be accessed from our web site at www. computer.org/cspress.

IPv6 Neighbor Discovery

Based on Linux Kernel 2.6.34

by Sameer Seth and M. Ajaykumar

IEEE ReadyNotes Series

IEEE Φ.computer society

Page design by Monette Velasco.

ISBN-10: 0-7695-4665-X
ISBN-13: 978-0-7695-4665-0
IEEE Computer Society Order Number: P4665

Contents

IPv6 Neighbor Discovery

T his document covers the "Address Resolution" feature of IPv6 Neighbor Discovery (ND). IPv6 ND has multiple functionalities. We will cover the following:

- IPv6 Introduction.
- Neighbor Discovery introduction and functionality.
- Address Resolution using the ND feature Neighbor Solicitation and Neighbor Advertisement.
- Neighbor Solicitation Message format and Neighbor Advertisement Message format.
- Neighbor Solicitation and Neighbor Advertisement implementation.

IPv6, or IP version 6, is a new version of Internet protocol. This IPv6 protocol will replace the current IPv4 protocol. The primary difference is that IPv6 uses 128-bit addresses, compared to the 32-bit addresses used with IPv4. The IPv6 address uses a 128-bit hexadecimal addressing scheme, represented in eight combinations of four hexadecimal numbers, each separated by a colon.

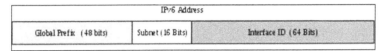

Figure 1. IPv6 Address Syntax

IPv6 Address Syntax

An IPv6 address consists of three fields:

Global Prefix: This is provided by the ISP, and its size is 48 bits.

Subnet: Its size is 16 bits, and it tells you to which particular organization this subnet ID belongs.

Interface ID: Its size is 64 bits, and this is either automatically generated from the 48-bit MAC address or assigned randomly or from a DHCPv6 server.

IPv6 Address Types:

Unicast Address: This address identifies a single network interface, and the packet is sent to this identified interface.

Multicast Address: This address identifies multiple network interfaces; a packet sent to the multicast address is delivered to all the interfaces identified by this address.

Anycast Address: This address identifies multiple network interfaces; a packet sent to an anycast address is delivered to one of the interfaces (the nearest interface identified by the address).

IPv6 Address Examples:

0:0:0:0:0:0:0:0—This is the equivalent of IPv4's 0.0.0.0
0:0:0:0:0:0:0:1—This is the equivalent of IPv4's 127.0.0.1
2000::/3—Global unicast address range
FC00::/7—Unique local unicast range
FE80::/10—Link-local unicast range
FF00::/8—Multicast range

For more information, please refer to RFC 4291—IP Version 6 Addressing Architecture.

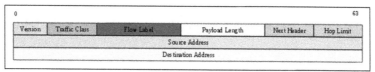

Figure 2. IPv6 Header Format

IP Header:

Version: This field indicates the version; it is IPv6. The size of this field is 4 bits.

Traffic Class: This field indicates the IPv6 packet's class or priority. The size of this field is 8 bits.

Flow Label: This field can be used by a source to label a set of packets belonging to the same flow. The size of this field is 20 bits.

Payload Length: This field indicates the length of the IPv6 payload, and this includes the extension headers. The size of this field is 16 bits.

Next Header: This field indicates either the type of the first extension header or the protocol in the upper layer protocol. The size of this field is 8 bits.

Hop Limit: This field is similar to the TTL field of IPv4. Its size is 8 bits.

Source Address: This field indicates the source address of the host. Its size is 128 bits.

Destination Address: This field indicates the target's destination address. Its size is 128 bits.

This section covers "IPv6 Neighbor Solicitation & Advertisement," which is one of the features of "IPv6 Neighbor Discovery." Figure 3 shows the path of packet outflow in IPv6 and the entry point in the network layer where it will check whether the neighbor's MAC address has already been resolved or not and, based on that result, calls the routines specific to the neighbor framework. In this document, our discussion will be specific to this neighbor framework.

Neighbor Discovery (ND) protocol in IPv6 is used by hosts and routers to identify and get information from the neighboring nodes (RFC 4861). Based on the information received, it decides the nature and reachability of neighboring nodes. ND protocol is part of ICMPv6. ND protocol is used to determine the link layer addresses of the neighbors, discovers the neighboring routers and checks the status of the neighbors.

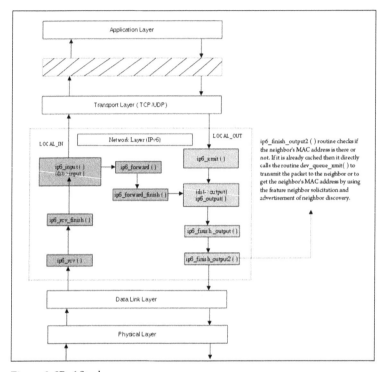

Figure 3. IPv6 Stack

IPv6 ND protocol replaces the following in IPv4:

- Address Resolution Protocol (ARP)
- Internet Control Message Protocol (ICMP) router Discovery & Redirect Message.

ND protocol also adds new functionality in IPv6. Following are the features supported:

- Address Auto Configuration
- Address Resolution
- Router Discovery
- Prefix Discovery
- Parameter Discovery
- Next Hop Determination

- Neighbor Unreachability Detection
- Duplicate Address Detection
- Redirect

Before proceeding further, we have to understand the few basic terminologies for IPv6 (see RFC 4861):

Node: Device which has IPv6 implementation.
Router: Node which will forward IPv6 packets not explicitly addressed to itself across networks.
Host: Device that is connected to a network and is not a router.
Neighbors: Nodes attached to the same link.

For more terminologies used, please refer to RFC 4861.

Various ND Protocol Functionalities:

Address Auto Configuration: This ND protocol functionality allows a node to auto-configure its own IPv6 address for interface based on the information available locally and from routers.

Address Resolution: This ND protocol functionality is used to resolve a destination node IPv6 address to its link layer (MAC) address.

Router Discovery: This ND protocol functionality allows a host to find or locate the routers on an attached link. This is similar to ICMPv4 router discovery.

Prefix Discovery: This ND protocol functionality allows hosts to discover the address prefixes for local link destinations.

Parameter Discovery: This ND protocol functionality allows a node to find link parameters, e.g., MTU (Maximum Transmission Unit) and the default hop limit for an outgoing packet.

Next Hop Determination: This ND protocol allows a node to determine the IPv6 address of the destination neighbor to which the packet should be sent. This destination neighbor can be a destination itself or a default router.

Neighbor Unreachability Detection: This ND protocol functionality allows a node to determine that a particular neighbor is no longer reachable.

Duplicate Address Detection: This ND protocol functionality is similar to Gratuitous ARP in IPv4. In this case a node determines that the IPv6 address it is using is not already in use by another node.

Redirect: This ND protocol functionality allows a router to inform a host of a better first-hop node to reach a destination. It is similar to the ICMPv4 Redirect message feature in IPv4.

Here, we are going to discuss only the Address Resolution functionality in IPv6 using Neighbor Discovery.

What is IPv6 Neighbor Discovery Address Resolution?
It is difficult to detect or identify any node using its IPv6 address, as it will not be the same and may change in the future. Each node is identified using its unique link layer (MAC) address.

For communication between hosts/nodes on the same or any network, address resolution plays an important role. If there is any failure in address resolution, there will not be any communication between hosts/nodes on any network.

The main functionality of Address Resolution is the same as Address Resolution Protocol (ARP) in IPv4:

• To resolve a destination node IPv6 address to its link layer (MAC) address. It also monitors for any change of events and reachability of the neighboring nodes.

For Address Resolution the Neighbor Discovery messages are:

• Neighbor Solicitation Message (ICMPv6 type 135)
• Neighbor Advertisement Message (ICMPv6 type 136)

To resolve the destination IPv6 address to its link layer address, the sending host sends a Multicast Neighbor Solicitation message on the network. The multicast destination link layer address from the ethernet header of the Neighbor Solicitation message is based on the IPv6 destination solicited node address. This solicited node address is derived from the destination IPv6 address. This message also contains the source link layer address.

On receiving the Multicast Neighbor Solicitation message, the target host/node retrieves the source link layer address and updates its neighbor cache. Then the target host/node sends a Unicast Neighbor Advertisement to the originator of the Neighbor Solicitation message with its link layer address. After receiving the Neighbor Advertisement message from the target host/node, the sending host/node retrieves the target's link layer address and updates its neighbor cache. Now the address resolution process is com-

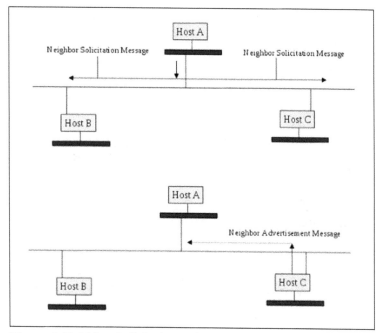

Figure 4. Neighbor Solicitation and Advertisement

plete, and the sending host/node and the target host/node can communicate successfully.

Neighbor Solicitation Message Format

The Ethernet Header consists of:

- The Destination field of the ethernet header is set to the destination Multicast Link Layer Address.
- The Source field of the ethernet header is set to the Source Link Layer Address of the sending host/node.
- The Type field of the ethernet header is set to IPv6.

The IPv6 header consists of:

- The Version field is set to 6, i.e., the IP version.
- The Payload Length field is set to 32, and it is the length of IPv6 payload.

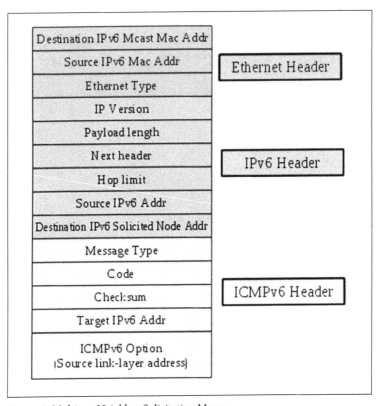

Destination IP v6 Mcast Mac Addr	
Source IPv6 Mac Addr	Ethernet Header
Ethernet Type	
IP Version	
Payload length	
Next header	IPv6 Header
Hop limit	
Source IPv6 Addr	
Destination IPv6 Solicited Node Addr	
Message Type	
Code	
Checksum	ICMPv6 Header
Target IPv6 Addr	
ICMPv6 Option (Source link-layer address)	

Figure 5. Multicast Neighbor Solicitation Message

- The Next Header field is set to ICMPv6, i.e., the extension header to access for information.
- The Hop Limit field is set to 255. This is the maximum number of routers the IPv6 packet can travel before being discarded.
- The Source Address field is set to the Source IPv6 address of the sending host.
- The Destination Address field is set to the solicited node address of the destination, which is derived from the destination IPv6 address.

The ICMPv6 Address consists of:

- The Type field is set to 135. It indicates the type of message; in this case, it is a Neighbor Solicitation message.

- The Code field is set to 0. It differentiates between multiple messages within a given message type. Here it is the only message for a given message type, so it is set to 0.
- The Checksum field is set to the checksum of the ICMPv6 message.
- The Target Address field is set to the destination/target IPv6 address.
- The ICMPv6 Option field is set to the Source link-layer address.

Neighbor Advertisement Message Format

The Ethernet Header consists of:

- The Destination field of the ethernet header is set to the Destination Link Layer Address.
- The Source field of the ethernet header is set to IPv6.

The IPv6 header consists of:

- The Version field is set to 6, i.e., the IP version.
- The Payload Length field is set to 32. It is the length of the IPv6 payload.
- The Next Header field is set to ICMPv6, i.e., the extension header to access for information.
- The Hop Limit field is set to 255. It is the maximum number of routers the IPv6 packet can travel before being discarded.
- The Source Address field is set to the Source IPv6 address of the sending host.
- The Destination Address field is set to the Destination IPv6 address.

The ICMPv6 Address consists of:

- The Type field is set to 136. It indicates the type of message; in this case, it is a Neighbor Advertisement message.
- The Code field is set to 0. It differentiates between multiple messages within a given message type. Here it is the only message for a given message type, so it is set to 0.
- The Checksum field is set to the checksum of the ICMPv6 message.
- The Flags field is set to indicate that this advertisement is in response to a solicitation message.
- The Target Address field is set to the IPv6 address being advertised.
- The ICMPv6 Option field is set to the Target link-layer address.

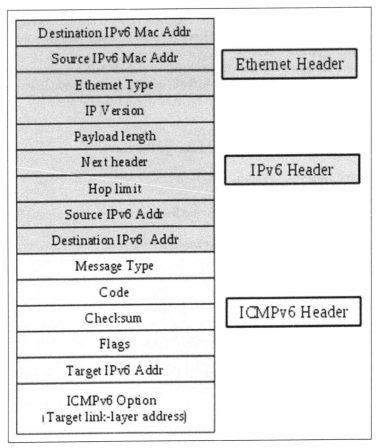

Figure 6. Neighbor Advertisement Message

Neighbor Table

Figure 7 shows the neighbor table implementation. The neighbor table contains the hardware address of neighbors and their status, with other relevant information such as device, IP address mapping, etc., that are on the same network as the host system. It is used as a cache, and the neighbor entries are not permanent. It is monitored with a timer and takes the specific action of updating the entries or deleting the entries based on timer expiry and reachability of neighbor. It also maintains the state of neighbor entries. This table has no entries if there is no communication between neighbors.

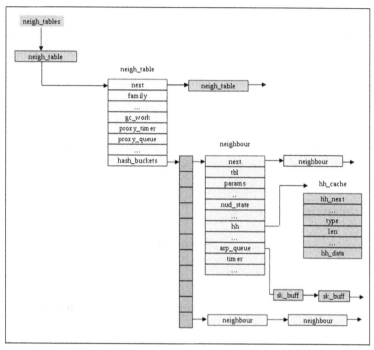

Figure 7. Neighbor Table Implementation

struct neighbor

This structure contains information about neighbor system. Some of the important fields of this structure are:

next: pointer to the next neighbor structure.

tbl: pointer to the neigh_table which represents the neighbor table in system.

params: pointer to neigh_params struct which contains information about the different parameters used in neighbor protocol.

dev: pointer to the net_device structure.

used: this field is to find out when the entry was used recently.

flags: this field is used to identify whether the neighbor is a router.

nud_state: neighbor table maintains state for each entry to keep track of the status, whether reachable or not. This field indicates the state of a neighbor entry, e.g., NUD_NONE, NUD_REACHABLE, NUD_

FAILED, etc.

probes: maximum allowed number for failed solicitation attempts. If all the attempts are over and address resolution has still not happened, then NUD_FAILED state is set to the neighbor entry.

lock: protects the neighbor structure from multiple access or race conditions.

ha: hardware address based on the IP address.

hh: pointer to cached hardware address.

arp_queue: sk_buff queue waiting for the address resolution.

timer: timer used to monitor the neighbor table and take appropriate after action expiry.

struct neigh_table

This structure represents a neighbor protocol for the system. Some of the important fields are:

next: pointer to the next neighbor table.

lock: protects the neighbor structure from multiple access or race conditions.

hash_buckets: pointer to the neighbor's hash table for this neigh_table struct. The size of hash table is 32 buckets, based on hash_mask value.

gc_work: garbage collection timer that cleans up the entries which are failed.

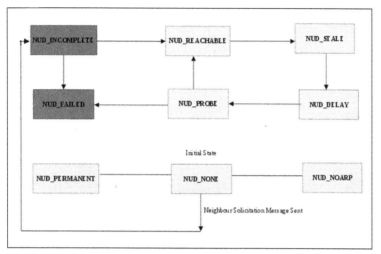

Figure 8. Neighbor State Diagram: Neighbor Advertisement Message Received

Neighbor States

NUD_NODE: New neighbor entry for neighbor cache will be in this state when created.

NUD_PERMANENT & NUD_NOARP: NUD_PERMANENT state is set by the administrator and is not deleted. NUD_NOARP state is used when no address resolution is required, e.g., PPP.

NUD_INCOMPLETE: There is no hardware address to use, so a Neighbor Solicitation request message has been sent and a reply is awaited.

NUD_REACHABLE: Neighbor Advertisement message is received, and the neighbor is reachable. Also, the hardware address of the neighbor is cached.

NUD_STALE: In this state, the neighbor is reachable, but the timer is expired, so the solicitation message will be sent again.

NUD_DELAY: In NUD_STALE, state if there is any communication to the neighbor, then the state will be set.

NUD_PROBE: If this state is set, then we are waiting for the Neighbor Advertisement message. It is thus in the probing state.

NUD_FAILED: If this state is set, then the address resolution has failed after the maximum number of tries, and this entry will be deleted.

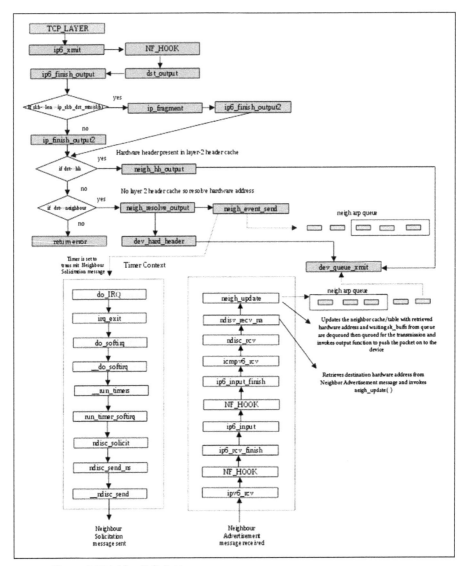

Figure 9. Neighbor Solicitation

Neighbor Solicitation

neigh_resolve_output ( )

The neigh_resolve_output ( ) routine (see code snippet 1) is indirectly invoked from the ip6_output_finish2( ) routine if the hardware address is not there in the destination entry (dst_entry struct). The main purpose of this routine is to get the target/destination MAC (link layer) address for the

Code snippet 1. neigh_resolve_output ( )

```
net/core/neighbor.c

1195 int neigh_resolve_output(struct sk_buff *skb)
1196 {
1197      struct dst_entry *dst = skb_dst(skb);
1198      struct neighbor *neigh;
1199      int rc = 0;
       . . .
1206      if (!neigh_event_send(neigh, skb)) {
1207           int err;
1208           struct net_device *dev = neigh->dev;
1209           if (dev->header_ops->cache && !dst->hh) {
1210                write_lock_bh(&neigh->lock);
1211                if (!dst->hh)
1212                     neigh_hh_init(neigh, dst,
                              dst->ops->protocol);
1213                err = dev_hard_header(skb, dev,
                         ntohs(skb->protocol),
1214                     neigh->ha, NULL, skb->len);
1215                write_unlock_bh(&neigh->lock);
1216           } else {
1217                read_lock_bh(&neigh->lock);
1218                err = dev_hard_header(skb, dev,
                         ntohs(skb->protocol),
1219                     neigh->ha, NULL, skb->len);
1220                read_unlock_bh(&neigh->lock);
1221           }
1222           if (err >= 0)
1223                rc = neigh->ops->queue_xmit(skb);
1224           else
1225                goto out_kfree_skb;
1226      }
1227 out:
1228      return rc;
       . . .
1236 }
```

target/destination IPV6 address. For this, it invokes the function neigh_event_send ( ) at line 1206.

_neigh_event_send( ) is a check routine for neighbor entries and will periodically monitor what needs to be done for the neighbor entries, whether a neighbor entry has exhausted its maximum tries to resolve the neighbor MAC address or the neighbor needs to be probed once again because it has already aged. This routine is not covered under the scope of this section but will be explained later.

This function returns zero if the neighbor state is any of these: NUD_

Code snippet 2. ndisc_solicit ( )

```
net/ipv6/ndisc.c

677 static void ndisc_solicit(struct neighbor *neigh,
                             struct sk_buff *skb)
678 {
679        struct in6_addr *saddr = NULL;
680        struct in6_addr mcaddr;
681        struct net_device *dev = neigh->dev;
682        struct in6_addr *target =(struct in6_addr *)
                                   &neigh->primary_key;
               . . .
684
685        if (skb && ipv6_chk_addr(dev_net(dev),
               &ipv6_hdr(skb)->saddr, dev, 1))
686            saddr = &ipv6_hdr(skb)->saddr;
               . . .
698        } else {
699            addrconf_addr_solict_mult(target,
                                          &mcaddr);
700            ndisc_send_ns(dev, NULL, target,
                                   &mcaddr, saddr);
701        }
702 }
```

CONNECTED, NUD_DELAY, or NUD_PROBE. If it is for the first time, a neighbor entry is newly created, and it is in NUD_NONE state, then neigh_event_send ( ) returns 1 and the "sk_buff" is queued in the neighbor structure's queue field. It will wait for the reply (for address resolution), then the "sk_buff" will be transmitted. If neigh_event_send ( ) returns 0, we have already resolved the neighbor. Then the control reaches line 1207.

Lines 1209–1211 check if the device has hard_header_cache function and doesn't have hh cache pointer. In that case, neigh_hh_init ( ) function is called at line 1212 with neigh lock held and bottomhalf disabled. We are disabling sofirq for this duration, as the interrupt path may execute softirq and may modify neighbor structure. This neigh lock is of type "rwlock_t structure," and we are acquiring the lock in write mode. This "rwlock_t" also protects the neighbor structure from race conditions.

At line 1213, the dev_hard_header ( ) function is invoked to create the ethernet header for the "sk_buff." It does this by invoking the eth_header ( ) routine. The target hardware header is passed as an argument to the dev_hard_header ( ) routine, and the source hardware header will be copied from the net_device, since it is passed as a NULL argument to dev_hard_header( ). In case of the hh cache pointer already being present,

```
Code snippet 3. ndisc_send_ns ( )

net/ipv6/ndisc.c

608 void ndisc_send_ns(struct net_device *dev,
                      struct neighbor *neigh,
609                   const struct in6_addr *solicit,
610                   const struct in6_addr *daddr,
                      const struct in6_addr *saddr)
611 {
612     struct in6_addr  addr_buf;
613     struct icmp6hdr icmp6h = {
614       .icmp6_type = NDISC_NEIGHBOR_SOLICITATION,
615     };
616
617     if (saddr == NULL) {
618             if (ipv6_get_lladdr(dev, &addr_buf,
619               (IFA_F_TENTATIVE|IFA_F_OPTIMISTIC)))
620                 return;
621             saddr = &addr_buf;
622     }
623
624     __ndisc_send(dev, neigh, daddr, saddr,
625             &icmp6h, solicit,
626             !ipv6_addr_any(saddr) ?
                    ND_OPT_SOURCE_LL_ADDR : 0);
627 }
```

then the dev_hard_header( ) routine is directly invoked with neigh lock in read mode at lines 1217–1218, and the ethernet header is created for the "sk_buff."

If there are no errors from the dev_hard_header ( ) routine, then we directly invoke neigh->ops->queue_xmit pointer, i.e., dev_queue_xmit( ), for transmission of "sk_buff" at line 1223.

ndisc_solicit ( )

The ndisc_solicit ( ) function (see code snippet 2) is scheduled to be invoked by the neigh_timer_handler ( ) routine. The purpose of this function is to send the Neighbor Solicitation request to obtain the target/destination MAC address. Variable "target" at line 682 holds the target/destination neighbor's IPv6 address. "skb" is passed as one of the arguments to this function. At lines 685–686, we verify this skb and validate the source IPv6 address. Then the "saddr" variable holds this source IP address. At line 699, the addrconf_addr_solicit_multi ( ) routine is invoked to derive the solicited node address (multicast MAC address) of the target neighbor from

```
Code snippet 4. __ndisc_send ( )

net/ipv6/ndisc.c

555 static void __ndisc_send(struct net_device *dev,
556                          struct neighbor *neigh,
557                          const struct in6_addr *daddr,
558                          const struct in6_addr *saddr,
559                          struct icmp6hdr *icmp6h,
                             const struct in6_addr *target,
560                          int llinfo)
561 {
562      struct sk_buff *skb;
563
564      skb = ndisc_build_skb(dev, daddr, saddr,
                    icmp6h, target, llinfo);
565      if (!skb)
566          return;
567
568      ndisc_send_skb(skb, dev, neigh, daddr,
                         saddr, icmp6h);
569 }
```

the target neighbor's IPv6 address, which then will be passed as a "mcaddr" argument to the ndisc_send_ns( ) function. Finally, ndisc_send_ns ( ) is called to send the Neighbor Solicitation request to the target neighbor's IPv6 address.

ndisc_send_ns ( )

The ndisc_send_ns( ) function (see code snippet 3) is invoked by the ndisc_solicit( ) routine. The main purpose of this function is to send the Neighbor Solicitation request. At lines 613–614, it initializes "icmp6hdr" type to "NDISC_NEIGHBOR_SOLICITATION," indicating that this is an ICMPv6 Neighbor Solicitation request message. At lines 617–621, in a case where "saddr" is NULL, ipv6_get_lladdr ( ) is called to assign the source address from the address list of the net device. Next is to call the routine __ndisc_send ( ) at line 624; this routine finally builds the ICMPv6 header and "sk_buff" and sends the Neighbor Discover packet to the target.

__ndisc_send ( )

The __ndisc_send ( ) function (see code snippet 4) is invoked by the ndisc_send_ns ( ) routine. The main purpose of this function is to build the "sk_buff" and send the Neighbor Discover packet to the target. To do this, at line 564 it invokes the ndisc_build_skb ( ) routine. This ndisc_build_skb ( )

Code snippet 5. ndisc_build_skb ( )

```
net/ipv6/ndisc.c

441  struct sk_buff *ndisc_build_skb(struct net_device *dev,
442                         const struct in6_addr *daddr,
443                         const struct in6_addr *saddr,
444                         struct icmp6hdr *icmp6h,
445                         const struct in6_addr *target,
446                         int llinfo)
447  {
448      struct net *net = dev_net(dev);
449      struct sock *sk = net->ipv6.ndisc_sk;
450      struct sk_buff *skb;
451      struct icmp6hdr *hdr;
452      int len;
453      int err;
454      u8 *opt;
458
459      len = sizeof(struct icmp6hdr) +
                  (target ? sizeof(*target) : 0);
460      if (llinfo)
461              len += ndisc_opt_addr_space(dev);
463      skb = sock_alloc_send_skb(sk,
464              (MAX_HEADER + sizeof(struct ipv6hdr) +
465              len + LL_ALLOCATED_SPACE(dev)),
473
474      skb_reserve(skb, LL_RESERVED_SPACE(dev));
475      ip6_nd_hdr(sk, skb, dev, saddr, daddr,
                  IPPROTO_ICMPV6, len);
477      skb->transport_header = skb->tail;
478      skb_put(skb, len);
```

continued...

routine builds the "sk_buff" using the arguments "daddr,""saddr,""icmp6h,"
"target," etc. Once the "sk_buff" is built and ready, then the ndisc_send_skb
( ) routine is called at line 568 with "sk_buff" as one of the arguments. This
ndisc_send_skb( ) routine is finally responsible for sending the Neighbor
Discover packet to the target. We will see more about how the "sk_buff" is
built using the ndisc_build_skb( ) routine in the next section.

ndisc_build_skb ( )
The ndisc_build_skb ( ) function (see code snippet 5) is called from the
__ndisc_send ( ) routine. The main purpose of this routine is to build and
initialize the "sk_buff" structure and also to calculate the space required for

```
Code snippet 6. ndisc_build_skb( ) (continued)

net/ipv6/ndisc.c

480        hdr = (struct icmp6hdr *)
                         skb_transport_header(skb);
481        memcpy(hdr, icmp6h, sizeof(*hdr));
482
483        opt = skb_transport_header(skb) +
                      sizeof(struct icmp6hdr);
484        if (target) {
485            ipv6_addr_copy((struct in6_addr *)opt,
                            target);
486            opt += sizeof(*target);
487        }
488
489        if (llinfo)
490            ndisc_fill_addr_option(opt, llinfo,
                                   dev->dev_addr,
491                                   dev->addr_len,
                                   dev->type);
492
493        hdr->icmp6_cksum = csum_ipv6_magic(saddr,
                                   daddr, len,
494                                   IPPROTO_ICMPV6,
495                                   csum_partial(hdr,
496                                       len, 0));
497
498        return skb;
499 }
```

the ICMPv6 header and extended ICMPv6 option. At line 459, the variable "len" is assigned a value equal to the sum of the size of the ICMPv6 header and the target/destination MAC address length. Then, at line 460–461, if "llinfo" is set, then the "len" variable is again modified with the new value, which is the sum of the size of the ICMPv6 header, the target/destination MAC address length, and the ICMPv6 option space required for the source link layer address. At line 463, we allocate the "sk_buff" structure or "skb" by calling the routine sock_alloc_send_skb( ). Then, at lines 474–475, skb_reserve( ) is invoked to adjust the headroom of an empty "sk_buff" or "skb," and then the IPv6 header is built and initialized by calling the routine ip6_nd_hdr( ).

In lines 480–481 (see code snippet 6), variable "hdr," which is a type of "icmp6hdr" structure, now points to transport_header of "sk_buff" structure or "skb." Then, using memcpy( ), the actual "icmp6hdr" that passed as

Code snippet 7. ndisc_send_skb ( )

```
net/ipv6/ndisc.c

503 void ndisc_send_skb(struct sk_buff *skb,
504                     struct net_device *dev,
505                     struct neighbor *neigh,
506                     const struct in6_addr *daddr,
507                     const struct in6_addr *saddr,
508                     struct icmp6hdr *icmp6h)
509 {
510     struct flowi fl;
511     struct dst_entry *dst;
512     struct net *net = dev_net(dev);
513     struct sock *sk = net->ipv6.ndisc_sk;
514     struct inet6_dev *idev;
515     int err;
516     u8 type;
517
518     type = icmp6h->icmp6_type;
519
520     icmpv6_flow_init(sk, &fl, type, saddr,
                         daddr, dev->ifindex);
521
522     dst = icmp6_dst_alloc(dev, neigh, daddr);
            . . .
527
            . . .
539     err = NF_HOOK(PF_INET6, NF_INET_LOCAL_OUT,
                      skb, NULL, dst->dev,
540                   dst_output);
            . . .
548 }
```

an argument to this routine will be copied to "hdr," so now the transport_
header of "skb" will contain the "icmpv6hdr." In lines 483–487, now "skb"
has the transport_header that is the ICMPv6 header. We have to copy the
target destination address at the end of the ICMPv6 header, so variable "opt"
is initialized to point to the immediate address after the icmpv6 header. Then
we copy the target destination address to this immediate address after the
ICMPv6 header. In lines 489–491, ndisc_fill_addr_option( ) is invoked to
initialize and copy the contents for ICPv6 option immediately after the IC-
MPv6 header and target destination address. In lines 493–496, the csum_
ipv6_magic( ) routine is called to calculate and assign the checksum for this
ICMPv6 header. Finally, at line 498 we return this "skb" or "sk_buff" structure to the __ndisc_send ( ) routine.

Code snippet 8. icmpv6_rcv ( )

net/ipv6/icmp.c

```
625 static int icmpv6_rcv(struct sk_buff *skb)
626 {
627         struct net_device *dev = skb->dev;
628         struct inet6_dev *idev = __in6_dev_get(dev);
629         struct in6_addr *saddr, *daddr;
630         struct ipv6hdr *orig_hdr;
631         struct icmp6hdr *hdr;
632         u8 type;
            . . .
679         hdr = icmp6_hdr(skb);
680
681         type = hdr->icmp6_type;
            . . .
685         switch (type) {
            . . .
717         case NDISC_ROUTER_SOLICITATION:
718         case NDISC_ROUTER_ADVERTISEMENT:
719         case NDISC_NEIGHBOR_SOLICITATION:
720         case NDISC_NEIGHBOR_ADVERTISEMENT:
721         case NDISC_REDIRECT:
722                 ndisc_rcv(skb);
723                 break;
            . . .
765         return 0;
766 }
```

ndisc_send_skb ( )

The ndisc_send_skb ( ) routine (see code snippet 7) is called by the __ndisc_send( ) function after a successful return from the ndisc_build_skb( ) routine. This routine is finally responsible for sending the neighbor discover packet to the target/destination address. We start with assigning the ICMPv6 type, which is nothing but the Neighbor Solicitation request message, to the "type" variable at line 518. Then we call the function icmpv6_flow_init( ) at line 520 to initialize the "flowi" struct with the arguments passed. At line 522, icmp6_dst_alloc ( ) will be called, which allocates the "dst_entry" structure and creates the neigh table for this specific multicast destination address and sets the multicast ethernet address in the neigh table by calling the function ndisc_get_neigh ( ), which again calls __neigh_lookup_errno( ). This __neigh_lookup_errno( ) in turn calls the neigh_create( ) routine, which invokes the function pointer "tbl->constructor," or ndisc_constructor ( ). In this ndisc_constructor( ) routine, ndisc_mc_map( ) is

```
Code snippet 9. ndisc_rcv ( )

net/ipv6/ndisc.c

1642 int ndisc_rcv(struct sk_buff *skb)
1643 {
1644     struct nd_msg *msg;
         . . .
1649     msg = (struct nd_msg *)
               skb_transport_header(skb);
         . . .
1669     switch (msg->icmph.icmp6_type) {
1670     case NDISC_NEIGHBOR_SOLICITATION:
1671          ndisc_recv_ns(skb);
1672          break;
1673
1674     case NDISC_NEIGHBOR_ADVERTISEMENT:
1675          ndisc_recv_na(skb);
1676          break;
         . . .
1691     return 0;
1692 }
```

called, which updates the "neigh_ha" field of the neighbor struct, which is nothing but the destination ethernet address. In this way, the target/destination MAC address is set. Finally, NF_HOOK( ) is called at line 539, which calls the function dst_output ( ).

icmpv6_rcv ( )

The net_rx_action( ) routine invokes the icmpv6_rcv ( ) routine when a Neighbor Discover packet is received (see code snippet 8). In this case, it's a Neighbor Advertisement message. At line 679, we get the ICMPv6 header address from the received "skb" or "sk_buff" structure. We assign this address to the "hdr" variable, which is of the type icmp6hdr structure. Then we retrieve the "ICMPv6 message type" from the ICMPv6 header and assign it to the "type" variable at line 681. Based on the type (in this case it is "NDISC_NEIGHBOR_ADVERTISEMENT"), we call the function ndisc_rcv ( ) at line 722.

ndisc_rcv ( )

The ndisc_rcv ( ) routine (see code snippet 9) is called from the icmpv6_rcv ( ) function. It basically checks the message type and, based on the message type, calls the specific neighbor function. At lines 1670–1672, this is related

```
Code snippet 10. ndisc_recv_na ( )

net/ipv6/ndisc.c

  897 static void ndisc_recv_na(struct sk_buff *skb)
  898 {
  899     struct nd_msg *msg = (struct nd_msg *)
                                 skb_transport_header(skb);
  900     struct in6_addr *saddr = &ipv6_hdr(skb)->saddr;
  901     struct in6_addr *daddr = &ipv6_hdr(skb)->daddr;
  902     u8 *lladdr = NULL;
  903     u32 ndoptlen = skb->tail -
                          (skb->transport_header +
  904                      offsetof(struct nd_msg, opt));
  905     struct ndisc_options ndopts;
  906     struct net_device *dev = skb->dev;
  907     struct inet6_ifaddr *ifp;
  908     struct neighbor *neigh;
      . . .
  929     if (!ndisc_parse_options(msg->opt, ndoptlen,
              &ndopts)) {
  934         if (ndopts.nd_opts_tgt_lladdr) {
  935             lladdr = ndisc_opt_addr_data
                      (ndopts.nd_opts_tgt_lladdr, dev);
  940         }
  941     }
  964     neigh = neigh_lookup(&nd_tbl, &msg->target,
              dev);
  985         neigh_update(neigh, lladdr,
  986             msg->icmph.icmp6_solicited ?
                  NUD_REACHABLE : NUD_STALE,
  987             NEIGH_UPDATE_F_WEAK_OVERRIDE |
  988             (msg->icmph.icmp6_override ?
                  NEIGH_UPDATE_F_OVERRIDE : 0) |
  989             NEIGH_UPDATE_F_OVERRIDE_ISROUTER |
  990             (msg->icmph.icmp6_router ?
                  NEIGH_UPDATE_F_ISROUTER : 0));
```

to receiving the Neighbor Solicitation request from the source destination and, in response to that, sending the Neighbor Advertisement request to the source destination. We will discuss this in the Neighbor Advertisement section. At line 1649, the "msg" variable, which is of type "nd_msg" structure, gets the pointer to transport_header of the received "skb" or "sk_buff" structure. Based on the ICMPv6 message type at line 1669 (in this case it's a Neighbor Advertisement message), it calls the routine ndisc_recv_na( ).

Code snippet 11. neigh_update ( )

```
net/core/neighbor.c

  985 int neigh_update(struct neighbor *neigh,
                       const u8 *lladdr, u8 new,
  986                  u32 flags)
  987 {
  988         u8 old;
  989         int err;
  990         int notify = 0;
  991         struct net_device *dev;
  992         int update_isrouter = 0;
          . . .
 1020         if (!dev->addr_len) {
              . . .
 1022             lladdr = neigh->ha;
 1023         } else if (lladdr) {
                  . . .
 1029             if ((old & NUD_VALID) &&
 1030                 !memcmp(lladdr,
                            neigh->ha, dev->addr_len))
 1031                     lladdr = neigh->ha;
 1032         } else {
                  . . .
 1036             err = -EINVAL;
 1037             if (!(old & NUD_VALID))
 1038                     goto out;
 1039             lladdr = neigh->ha;
 1040         }
              . . .
```

continued...

ndisc_recv_na ( )

The ndisc_recv_na ( ) routine (see code snippet 10) is called from the ndisc_ rcv ( ) routine. It receives the Neighbor Advertisement message from the target destination in response to the Neighbor Solicitation message. In lines 929–935, we retrieve the target MAC (link layer) address from the received "skb" or "sk_buff" structure. First we copy the address of transport header from "skb" to the "msg" variable, which is of type "nd_msg" structure. This transport header is the ICMPv6 message of type Neighbor Advertisement. It consists of the ICMPv6 message, the target IPv6 destination address, and

```
Code snippet 11a. neigh_update ( ) (continued)


1078
1079        if (lladdr != neigh->ha) {
1080                memcpy(&neigh->ha, lladdr,
                           dev->addr_len);
1081                neigh_update_hhs(neigh);
              . . .
1087     if (new == old)
1088             goto out;
1089     if (new & NUD_CONNECTED)
1090             neigh_connect(neigh);
1091     else
1092             neigh_suspect(neigh);
              . . .
1098                while (neigh->nud_state &
                           NUD_VALID &&
1099                 (skb = __skb_dequeue
                      (&neigh->arp_queue))
                        != NULL) {
1100                  struct neighbor *n1 = neigh;
              . . .
1103                  if (skb_dst(skb) &&
                         skb_dst(skb)->neighbor)
1104                   n1 = skb_dst(skb)->neighbor;
1105                  n1->output(skb);
              . . .
1107                }
1108                skb_queue_purge(&neigh->arp_queue);
1109          }
          . . .
1121      return err;
1122 }
```

the ICMPv6 option message. This ICMPV6 option message is of the type "Target link-layer address," i.e., it contains the target link layer address. The ndisc_parse_options( ) routine parses the ICMPv6 option message, and finally we can retrieve the target MAC (link layer) address from this ICMPv6 message by calling the function ndisc_opt_addr_data ( ) in "lladdr" variable. At line 985, this routine invokes the neigh_update ( ) routine to update the neighbor cache.

neigh_update ( ):
The neigh_update ( ) routine (see code snippet 11) is called from the ndisc_recv_na ( ) routine. It updates the neighbor cache with the link layer (MAC)

address of the target destination and the state. At lines 1020–1022, if the new state is VALID and the device address length is zero, then the "lladdr" variable is set to the neighbor structure's "ha" field, which is also zero in this case. At line 1029–1031, if the old state is valid, then the new hardware address is compared to the cached hardware address. If both are equal, then the "lladdr" variable is set to the present hardware address from the cache. At lines 1032–1039, if no address is specified, then the "err" variable is set to "EINVAL." Then, if the old entry is still VALID, the present hardware address from the cache is used.

At lines 1079–1081 (see code snippet 11a), the new link layer address or "lladdr" is copied to the neighbor hardware address field using memcpy(). Then all of the neighbor cache entry is updated by calling the function neigh_update_hhs ( ). At lines 1087–1092, if the state is not changed and it is in CONNECTED state, then neigh_connect ( ) is called to set up the fast transmit path; otherwise, the slow path is set up by calling the function neigh_suspect ( ). At lines 1098–1108, if the new state is a VALID state, then sk_buffs are waiting to be transmitted on the queue, so now these sk_buffs are dequeued and queued for the transmission. For this, the output function n1->output is invoked to push the packet on to the device after setting up the hardware header. Finally, the queue is purged after dequeueing the sk_buffs.

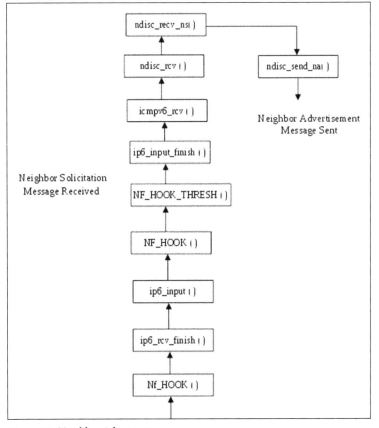

Figure 10. Neighbor Advertisement

Neighbor Advertisement

ndisc_recv_ns ( )

The ndisc_recv_ns ( ) routine (see code snippet 12) is called from the ndisc_rcv ( ) routine. It receives the Neighbor Solicitation message from the source destination to process this Neighbor Solicitation request for the MAC (link layer) address and to send Neighbor Advertisement to the source destination in response to the Solicitation request. In lines 756–768, we retrieve the source MAC (link layer) address from the received "skb" or "sk_ buff" structure. First we copy the address of the transport header from "skb"

Code snippet 12. ndisc_recv_ns ( )

net/ipv6/ndisc.c

```
719 static void ndisc_recv_ns(struct sk_buff *skb)
720 {
721         struct nd_msg *msg = (struct nd_msg *)
                                skb_transport_header(skb);
722         struct in6_addr *saddr = &ipv6_hdr(skb)->saddr;
723         struct in6_addr *daddr = &ipv6_hdr(skb)->daddr;
724         u8 *lladdr = NULL;
725         u32 ndoptlen = skb->tail -
                            (skb->transport_header +
726                         offsetof(struct nd_msg, opt));
727         struct ndisc_options ndopts;
728         struct net_device *dev = skb->dev;
729         struct inet6_ifaddr *ifp;
730         struct inet6_dev *idev = NULL;
731         struct neighbor *neigh;
732         int dad = ipv6_addr_any(saddr);
733         int inc;
734         int is_router = -1;
               . . .
756         if (!ndisc_parse_options(msg->opt,
               ndoptlen, &ndopts)) {
757             . . .
760         }
761
762         if (ndopts.nd_opts_src_lladdr) {
763             lladdr = ndisc_opt_addr_data
                       (ndopts.nd_opts_src_lladdr, dev);
764             . . .
768             }
```

continued...

to the "msg" variable, which is of type "nd_msg" structure. This transport header is the ICMPv6 message of type Neighbor Solicitation. It consists of the ICMPv6 message, the target IPv6 destination address, and the ICMPv6 option message. This ICMPv6 option message is of type "Source link-layer address," i.e., it contains the source link layer address. The ndisc_parse_options ( ) routine parses the ICMPv6 option message, and finally we can retrieve the source MAC (link layer) address from this ICMPv6 message by calling the function ndisc_opt_addr_data ( ) in "lladdr" variable.

At lines 874–879 (see code snippet 12a), we check for the neighbor entry

---

Code snippet 12a. ndisc_recv_ns ( ) (continued)

net/ipv6/ndisc.c

```
865        if (inc)
866                NEIGH_CACHE_STAT_INC(&nd_tbl,
                               rcv_probes_mcast);
867        else
868                NEIGH_CACHE_STAT_INC(&nd_tbl,
                               rcv_probes_ucast);
869

           . . .
874        neigh = __neigh_lookup(&nd_tbl, saddr,
                              dev,
875                           !inc || lladdr
                              || !dev->addr_len);
876        if (neigh)
877            neigh_update(neigh, lladdr,
                       NUD_STALE,
878                   NEIGH_UPDATE_F_WEAK_OVERRIDE|
879                   NEIGH_UPDATE_F_OVERRIDE);
880        if (neigh || !dev->header_ops) {
881            ndisc_send_na(dev, neigh, saddr,
                       &msg->target,
882                    is_router,
883                    1, (ifp != NULL && inc), inc);
884            if (neigh)
885                neigh_release(neigh);
886        }
           . . .
894        return;
895 }
```

---

in the neigh table by calling the neigh_lookup ( ) routine. Otherwise, it will create the new neighbor entry for this request. If the neighbor entry is there, then this routine invokes the neigh_update ( ) routine to update the neighbor cache at line 877. At lines 880–881, after updating the neighbor cache with the source IPv6 address and the link layer address, we have to send the Neighbor Advertisement request in response to the Neighbor Solicitation request from the source destination, so we finally send the Neighbor Advertisement request at line 881 by invoking the routine ndisc_send_na ( ). In this way we respond to the Neighbor Solicitation request from the source destination.

Summary

- IPv6 ND feature "Neighbor Solicitation and Advertisement" replaces the "IPv4 Address Resolution Protocol" in IPv6.
- To resolve the destination IPv6 address to its link layer address, the sending host sends a Multicast Neighbor Solicitation message on the network.
- On receiving the Multicast Neighbor Solicitation message, the target host/node updates its neighbor cache and sends a Unicast Neighbor Advertisement message to the originator of the Neighbor Solicitation message with its link address.
- IPv6 ND uses ICMPv6 to provide the functionality of ARP.
- IPv6 ND uses the same neighbor framework (timer, states, etc.) as ARP in IPv4.
- For Address Resolution, the ND messages are:

  - Neighbor Solicitation Message (ICMPv6 type 135)
  - Neighbor Advertisement Message (ICMPv6 type 136)

References

LXR, "The Linux Cross Reference," http://lxr.linux.no.

RFC 2460: S. Deering et al., "Internet Protocol Vertical 6 (IPv6) Specification," 1998, http://tools.ietf.org/html/rfc2460.

RFC 3513: R. Hindin et al., "Internet Protocol Version 6 (IPv6) Addressing Architecture," 2003, http://tools.ietf.org/html/rfc3513.

RFC 4291: R. Hindin et al., "Internet Protocol Version 6 Addressing Architecture," 2006, http://tools.ietf.org/html/rfc4291.

RFC 4443: A. Conta et al., "Internet Control Message Protocol (ICMPv6)," 2006, http://tools.ietf.org/html/rfc4443.

RFC 4861: T. Narten et al., "Neighbor Discovery for IP version 6 (Ipv6)," 2007, http://tools.ietf.org/html/rfc4861.